Evergreen Employment

Unveiling Timeless Job Wisdom

*The Ultimate Guide to Finding Your Path
in the Historical Tapestry of Work*

Written by

Morgan E. Blake

Independently published

2024

Introduction: The Timeless Journey of Employment

The Evolution of Work

The story of work is as old as humanity itself. From the earliest days of civilization, work has been a cornerstone of human existence. It's a tale that intertwines with our very evolution, shaping societies, cultures, and economies. This journey, from primitive beginnings to the sophisticated employment landscape of today, offers profound insights into not just our past, but also our present and future.

In the **dawn of time**, work was primarily about survival. Our ancestors, the hunter-gatherers, engaged in work as a means to feed, shelter, and protect their communities. This period was characterized by a direct and immediate connection between effort and reward—a concept still relevant in today's job market, albeit in a more complex form.

With the advent of agriculture, work underwent its first major transformation. The **Agricultural Revolution** marked a shift from nomadic lifestyles to settled farming communities. This era saw the birth of structured labor, the division of tasks, and the beginnings of trade. Here, the seeds of modern employment were sown, as people began to specialize in specific roles—a precursor to today's career specialization.

The Industrial Revolution was the next significant milestone. This period revolutionized work, introducing machinery, factories, and mass production. It marked a departure from artisanal, handcrafted goods to mass-produced items. The factory system not only changed the nature of work but also led to the development of new social classes and the urbanization of society. It's during this era that concepts like employment contracts, wages, and working hours began to take shape, forming the bedrock of contemporary employment law and practices.

Fast forward to the 20th century, and we witness the birth of the **Digital Age**. The advent of computers and the internet has transformed work in ways unimaginable a century ago. The digital revolution has democratized information, globalized economies, and created new industries. Today, we talk about digital nomads, telecommuting, and e-commerce—terms that were inconceivable in the pre-digital era.

In the current landscape, the concept of work is continuously evolving. We're seeing the rise of the gig economy, remote working, and artificial intelligence. These changes are not just technological but cultural, reflecting a shift in values and priorities. The modern worker values flexibility, work-life balance, and meaningful employment—trends that are reshaping the job market.

But what remains evergreen, through all these transformations, is the intrinsic human drive to work. Work gives us purpose, a sense of identity, and a means to contribute to society. This essence of work, this timeless wisdom, is what connects us to our ancestors and will continue to do so for generations to come.

In the next chapters, we will delve deeper into these changes, exploring how they impact the way we view and approach work today. From the early beginnings and the Industrial Revolution to the Digital Age and modern work dynamics, each era has contributed to the tapestry of employment, weaving a story rich with lessons and insights.

As we navigate through the historical journey of work, remember, it's not just about understanding the past. It's about using this knowledge to shape our future in the world of work—a future that's as ever-changing as it is evergreen.

Understanding the 'Evergreen' Concept in Employment

In exploring the realm of employment, one encounters the concept of **'evergreen employment.'** This idea, much like the perennial evergreen trees that retain their leaves throughout the seasons, refers to career strategies and job roles that remain relevant, valuable, and in demand regardless of economic fluctuations, technological advancements, or changing social trends.

To fully grasp this concept, consider the nature of the evergreen tree. It adapts to its environment, withstands seasonal changes, and remains steadfast and resilient through various climatic challenges. Similarly, **evergreen employment strategies** are those that adapt to the ever-changing job market while maintaining their core value. They are not swayed by temporary trends or short-lived demands but are rooted in enduring principles of the working world.

One of the fundamental aspects of evergreen employment is **versatility**. In a landscape marked by rapid technological changes and evolving job descriptions, versatility becomes a prized asset. It's about having a skill set that's not only in demand today but can adapt to the needs of tomorrow. Skills like critical thinking, problem-solving, effective communication, and emotional intelligence are timeless in their utility and applicability across various industries and roles.

Another key element is the **continuous pursuit of knowledge and skills**. The evergreen professional understands that learning doesn't stop at graduation. In a world where new technologies emerge at a blistering pace and industries evolve continuously, ongoing education and skill development are crucial. This could mean formal education, self-taught skills, or on-the-job learning. The aim is to remain relevant and adaptable in a dynamic work environment.

Furthermore, an evergreen employment approach embraces **flexibility and adaptability** in career paths. Gone are the days when a career was a linear journey from one promotion to the next within a single company or industry. Today's evergreen professionals are open to lateral moves, new challenges, and sometimes even complete career changes. They recognize the value of diverse experiences and the breadth of skills and perspectives gained from them.

Networking and relationship-building are also integral to evergreen employment. In a world where opportunities often arise through connections, maintaining a robust professional network is invaluable. This doesn't just mean collecting contacts but nurturing meaningful relationships that can provide support, advice, and opportunities throughout one's career.

Embracing technology is another crucial aspect. Regardless of one's field, understanding and leveraging the latest technological tools and platforms is essential in today's job market. This could range from basic digital literacy to specialized technical skills, depending on the job role. The evergreen professional is not intimidated by new technologies but views them as tools to enhance productivity and open new doors.

Lastly, an evergreen approach to employment emphasizes **work-life balance and personal well-being**. In the relentless pursuit of career success, it's easy to overlook personal health and happiness. However, sustainable career growth is intrinsically linked to a healthy work-life balance. This includes setting boundaries, prioritizing mental and physical health, and ensuring that work enriches rather than depletes one's life.

In summary, understanding and adopting the evergreen concept in employment is about recognizing and cultivating these timeless qualities and strategies. It's a holistic approach, combining adaptability, continuous learning, versatility, networking, technological proficiency, and personal well-being. By embodying these principles, one can navigate the ever-changing job market with resilience and agility, much like the evergreen tree stands resilient through the changing seasons.

Chapter 1: Labor Through the Ages

Early Beginnings and the Industrial Revolution

Reflecting on the **early beginnings of labor**, it is clear that the journey of employment has been deeply intertwined with the evolution of human society. This journey, starting from the rudimentary barter systems of ancient civilizations to the structured economic systems of later periods, laid the groundwork for modern employment concepts. In these early societies, work was primarily about survival and community contribution. Every member of the community had a role, whether as a farmer, a craftsman, or a trader, and these roles were often passed down through generations, creating the first semblance of career lineage.

Agriculture played a pivotal role in these early stages. With the advent of farming, humans settled in one place, leading to the establishment of communities and the creation of structured work systems. This period was marked by a significant shift from nomadic lifestyles to settled agrarian communities, which brought about the need for organized labor and resource management.

However, the real transformation in the world of work began with the **Industrial Revolution**. This period, starting in the late 18th century, marked a dramatic shift from manual labor and artisanal crafts to mechanized production. It heralded the age of factories, where work became more regimented and centralized. The Industrial Revolution was not just a period of technological innovation; it was a time of profound social change. The factory system led to urbanization, as people moved from rural areas to cities in search of work. This migration changed the landscape of employment and the dynamics of the labor market significantly.

The Industrial Revolution also brought about a new class structure, with a clear demarcation between the working class and the industrial capitalists. Workers in factories often faced long hours, low wages, and unsafe working conditions. This led to the rise of labor movements and the fight for workers' rights, laying the foundation for modern labor laws and regulations.

One of the most significant aspects of the Industrial Revolution was the **standardization of work**. The introduction of assembly lines and factory systems meant that work could be broken down into smaller, repetitive tasks. This was a departure from the artisanal, skill-specific work of the past and led to the creation of a more general labor force. It also paved the way for the development of managerial roles and the hierarchical structure of modern organizations.

The technologies introduced during the Industrial Revolution, such as the steam engine and spinning jenny, not only transformed industries but also impacted the skills required for employment. There was a shift from artisanal skills to skills that could support and maintain the new machinery. This period saw the beginnings of vocational training and education systems designed to meet the needs of industrialized work.

As the Industrial Revolution progressed into the 19th and 20th centuries, it set the stage for further developments in the workplace, including the introduction of electricity, the telephone, and later, the computer. These technologies continued to transform the nature of work, leading to increased efficiency, the creation of new industries, and the evolution of existing ones.

In summary, the early beginnings of labor and the Industrial Revolution represent a significant era in the history of employment. It was a time of profound change, not just in the methods of production but in the very fabric of society. The legacy of this period is still felt today in the structures, systems, and laws that govern the modern workplace. Understanding this historical context is essential for appreciating the evolution of work and for navigating the current and future landscapes of employment. As we move forward in this book, we will explore how these early foundations have shaped the modern job market and what lessons we can draw from them in our pursuit of evergreen employment.

The Digital Age and Modern Work Dynamics

As we transition from the Industrial Revolution into **the Digital Age**, the landscape of work has undergone a seismic shift. This era, ushered in by the advent of computers and the Internet, has redefined not just the tools we use, but the very nature of our work. The Digital Age has created a paradigm shift in employment, from the types of jobs available to the ways in which we perform them.

The Dawn of the Digital Age began with the development of the first computers and digital networks in the mid-20th century. This period marked the start of a technological revolution that would eventually permeate every aspect of our lives, including our work. The early computers, massive and expensive, were initially used by governments and large corporations. However, as technology advanced, these machines became smaller, more affordable, and more powerful, eventually leading to the personal computer revolution of the 1980s and 1990s.

This era heralded the rise of the **information economy**, where information became just as valuable as physical goods. The ability to process, analyze, and transmit data rapidly and efficiently became a key driver of economic growth. In this new economy, knowledge workers – those who work primarily with information – became a vital part of the workforce.

The introduction of the **Internet** in the 1990s was another major milestone. It transformed the digital landscape by connecting computers globally, allowing for unprecedented levels of communication and information exchange. The Internet gave rise to new industries, such as e-commerce, digital marketing, and social media, creating a plethora of new job opportunities. It also enabled more traditional businesses to operate more efficiently and reach a global market.

One of the defining characteristics of the Digital Age is the **blurring of boundaries** between work and personal life. With the advent of smartphones and cloud computing, employees are no longer tethered to a physical office. Remote work, telecommuting, and digital nomadism have become increasingly common, offering flexibility and challenging traditional notions of the workplace.

The Digital Age has also seen the rise of the **gig economy**, where short-term, flexible jobs are commonplace. Platforms like Uber, Airbnb, and Freelancer.com have created new ways for people to earn income, offering flexibility and autonomy, but also raising questions about job security and benefits.

With these changes come new challenges. The Digital Age demands **continuous learning and adaptation**. Skills that were valuable a decade ago may be obsolete today. Professionals must continuously update their skills to stay relevant in a rapidly changing job market. This era also poses challenges in terms of data security, privacy, and the ethical use of technology.

Furthermore, the Digital Age has had a significant impact on **organizational structures**. Hierarchical models are giving way to more networked, team-based structures. Collaboration and agility have become key components of organizational success. Companies are increasingly valuing skills such as digital literacy, adaptability, and collaborative ability over traditional metrics like tenure and hierarchy.

In conclusion, the Digital Age has fundamentally altered the dynamics of work. It has created new opportunities and challenges, requiring a workforce that is adaptable, tech-savvy, and continuously learning. As we delve deeper into this age, it becomes increasingly clear that the principles of evergreen employment – adaptability, continuous learning, and resilience – are more relevant than ever. Understanding and navigating this new landscape is crucial for anyone looking to succeed in the modern job market. In the following chapters, we will explore how to harness the opportunities of the Digital Age, adapt to its challenges, and carve out a fulfilling and sustainable career path.

Chapter 2: The Pillars of Evergreen Employment

Adaptability in Changing Job Markets

In the ever-evolving landscape of employment, **adaptability** has emerged as a key attribute, almost a necessity, for thriving in the modern job market. The ability to adapt – to changing technologies, evolving industry standards, and shifting economic tides – is what separates those who flourish from those who flounder in their careers. In this chapter, we'll explore the facets of adaptability in the context of employment, shedding light on its importance and how it can be cultivated.

The Essence of Adaptability

Adaptability in the job market is not just about the ability to adjust to a new job or a different set of responsibilities. It's a more holistic concept, encompassing the readiness to learn new skills, the willingness to embrace change, and the resilience to navigate the uncertainties of the job landscape. It's about being agile in thought and action, being prepared to pivot when necessary, and being open to continuous personal and professional growth.

Why Adaptability Matters

In today's fast-paced world, industries are transforming at an unprecedented rate. What was relevant yesterday might be obsolete tomorrow. New technologies are emerging, old ones are being phased out, and the demand for certain skills is continually evolving. In such a scenario, adaptability becomes crucial. It's not just about keeping up with changes; it's about anticipating them and being proactive in one's approach to career development.

Cultivating Adaptability

Adaptability isn't an inherent trait but a skill that can be developed. It starts with a mindset that is open to change and willing to step out of comfort zones. Cultivating adaptability involves staying informed about industry trends, investing time and resources in continuous learning, and being flexible in one's approach to problem-solving and decision-making.

Learning and Unlearning

A significant aspect of adaptability is the ability to learn – and sometimes, unlearn – skills and knowledge. This requires staying abreast of emerging trends in your field and pursuing relevant education and training opportunities. Equally important is the ability to unlearn outdated practices and obsolete information, making room for newer, more relevant knowledge.

Embracing Technological Change

In the Digital Age, technological proficiency is a cornerstone of adaptability. Embracing new technologies, understanding their implications in your field, and acquiring the necessary skills to use them effectively are essential steps in remaining competitive and relevant.

Flexibility in Career Paths

Adaptability also means being open to varied career paths. The traditional linear career trajectory is becoming increasingly rare. Today's job market favors those who can pivot across different roles, industries, and even career types. This might mean changing careers entirely, transitioning to a different industry, or taking on diverse roles within the same organization.

Building a Network

Adaptability extends to one's professional network. Building and maintaining a diverse network of contacts can provide insights into emerging opportunities and trends, offer support during transitions, and open doors to new possibilities.

Resilience and Emotional Intelligence

Lastly, adaptability is closely linked to resilience – the ability to bounce back from setbacks – and emotional intelligence, which involves understanding and managing one's emotions and empathizing with others. These qualities are vital in navigating the ups and downs of a dynamic job market.

Conclusion

Adaptability in the job market is about being proactive, not reactive. It's about foreseeing changes and preparing oneself to meet them head-on. It's a continuous process of learning, unlearning, and relearning. By fostering adaptability, individuals can ensure that they not only survive but thrive in the ever-changing tapestry of work. As we move forward in this book, we will delve deeper into practical strategies and tools to enhance your adaptability in the job market, empowering you to navigate your career path with confidence and agility.

The Power of Continuous Learning

In the dynamic tapestry of today's employment landscape, **continuous learning** stands out as a beacon, guiding the way to career longevity and success. This concept transcends the traditional idea of education confined to the early years of one's life. Instead, it embraces a lifelong pursuit of knowledge and skills, adapting to the ever-evolving demands of the job market. The power of continuous learning is not just in acquiring new information; it's in fostering a mindset that values growth, adaptability, and resilience.

Why Continuous Learning is Crucial

In an age where technological advancements and industry shifts happen at breakneck speed, the half-life of skills is becoming shorter. What was relevant yesterday might not suffice tomorrow. Continuous learning is the key to staying relevant and competitive. It's about keeping pace with the latest trends, understanding new technologies, and developing skills that are in demand.

Building a Learning Culture

Creating a culture of continuous learning starts with a mindset shift. It's about moving away from viewing education as a finite phase and seeing it as a continuous journey. This means being proactive about seeking learning opportunities, whether through formal education, online courses, workshops, webinars, or self-directed learning.

Leveraging Technology for Learning

The Digital Age has transformed how we access knowledge. Online learning platforms, virtual classrooms, and digital resources have made education more accessible than ever. Utilizing these tools effectively can significantly enhance the learning experience, offering flexibility and a wealth of information at one's fingertips.

Customizing Your Learning Path

Continuous learning is not a one-size-fits-all approach. It involves customizing one's learning journey according to personal career goals, industry requirements, and individual learning styles. This might mean focusing on technical skills in one phase of your career and soft skills in another, or balancing between industry-specific knowledge and broader business acumen.

Integrating Learning into Daily Life

Making learning a part of everyday life is essential. This could mean setting aside time each day or week for study, listening to educational podcasts during commutes, or reading industry-related articles and books. The key is to create a habit of learning, making it a regular part of your routine.

Learning from Experience

Continuous learning also involves learning from on-the-job experiences. Every new project, challenge, or role is an opportunity to acquire new skills and insights. Reflecting on these experiences, both successes and failures, is a valuable part of the learning process.

Networking and Collaborative Learning

Learning is not an isolated activity. Engaging with professional networks, participating in industry groups, and collaborating with peers can provide significant learning opportunities. Sharing knowledge and experiences with others not only enhances your own learning but contributes to the collective knowledge of your professional community.

The Benefits of Continuous Learning

The benefits of continuous learning extend beyond just staying employable. It fuels personal growth, boosts confidence, and enhances creativity. It keeps you mentally active and engaged, opening doors to new opportunities and pathways you might not have considered otherwise.

Conclusion

Embracing continuous learning is to embrace a future of possibilities. It's about being prepared for the changes and challenges that lie ahead in the job market. As we continue on this journey through 'Evergreen Employment', the importance of continuously updating our skills and knowledge becomes increasingly clear. It's not just an investment in your career; it's an investment in yourself and your future. In the following chapters, we will explore practical strategies to integrate continuous learning into your career development plan, ensuring that your skills and knowledge remain as evergreen as your approach to employment.

Chapter 3: Crafting Your Career Path

Identifying Personal Strengths and Market Needs

At the core of forging a successful career path is the ability to identify and align one's **personal strengths** with the **needs of the market**. This process is a crucial step in the journey toward evergreen employment. It's about understanding yourself – your skills, passions, and values – and how these align with the opportunities and needs in the job market. This alignment is the cornerstone of not just finding a job, but building a fulfilling, resilient career.

Understanding Your Personal Strengths

Your personal strengths are the unique combination of skills, abilities, and personality traits that you bring to the table. Identifying these strengths is not always straightforward. It requires introspection and sometimes, feedback from peers, mentors, or coaches. Start by asking yourself some key questions: What tasks do you find effortless? What activities energize you? What are the skills that others consistently commend in you?

Reflect on your past experiences, both in professional and personal contexts. Consider moments when you felt most accomplished and analyze the skills and qualities that contributed to those successes. Utilizing tools like personality tests (e.g., Myers-Briggs, StrengthsFinder) can also provide valuable insights.

Aligning with Market Needs

Once you have a clear understanding of your strengths, the next step is to align them with market needs. This requires staying informed about the trends and demands in your chosen industry or field. Research the market, understand which skills are in high demand, and identify any gaps in your skill set.

In a rapidly evolving job market, certain skills are perennially in demand. These include problem-solving, critical thinking, emotional intelligence, and adaptability. Technical skills may vary greatly depending on the industry, but digital literacy is increasingly important across the board.

Bridging the Gap

If there's a gap between your strengths and market needs, consider it an opportunity for growth. This is where continuous learning plays a vital role. Whether it's taking up additional training, seeking mentorship, or gaining practical experience, there are numerous ways to develop the skills that are in demand.

Leveraging Your Unique Combination

Remember, it's not just about having a certain set of skills; it's about how you uniquely combine and apply them. This unique combination is what sets you apart in the job market. For instance, a graphic designer with excellent communication skills and a deep understanding of user experience will stand out more than one who focuses solely on technical design skills.

Staying Adaptable

In a dynamic job market, adaptability is key. Your strengths and the market needs might evolve over time, and staying adaptable means continuously reassessing and realigning these two aspects. Be open to exploring new roles, industries, or even career paths if they align better with your evolving strengths and interests.

Conclusion

Identifying and aligning your personal strengths with market needs is a dynamic and ongoing process. It requires self-awareness, an understanding of the job market, and a commitment to personal development. By mastering this alignment, you position yourself not just for employment, but for a fulfilling career that can withstand the test of time and change. In the upcoming sections, we will explore strategies for leveraging this alignment, ensuring that you not only find a job that fits but also carve a career path that truly resonates with your strengths and the evolving landscape of work.

Strategies for Long-Term Career Growth

In the journey of professional development, understanding and implementing **strategies for long-term career growth** is vital. This isn't just about climbing the corporate ladder; it's about creating a fulfilling, sustainable career that aligns with personal goals and market needs. Let's delve into the essential strategies that can guide you towards long-term success and satisfaction in your career.

1. Setting Clear Career Goals

The first step in long-term career planning is setting clear and achievable goals. These goals should be specific, measurable, attainable, relevant, and time-bound (SMART). Whether it's aspiring to reach a particular position, mastering a skill, or achieving work-life balance, having a clear vision provides direction and motivation. Periodically review and adjust these goals as needed to remain aligned with your personal growth and changes in the job market.

2. Continuous Skill Development

In an ever-evolving job market, the importance of continuous learning cannot be overstated. This includes both formal education and informal learning opportunities. Stay updated on the latest trends and technologies in your field, and be proactive in acquiring new skills. This might mean pursuing advanced degrees, certifications, online courses, or attending workshops and seminars.

3. Building a Strong Professional Network

Networking is crucial for long-term career growth. A robust professional network can provide support, mentorship, and access to unadvertised job opportunities. Attend industry conferences, join professional associations, and engage in online professional communities. Remember, effective networking is about building genuine relationships, not just exchanging business cards.

4. Seeking Feedback and Mentorship

Regular feedback is essential for professional growth. Seek constructive feedback from supervisors, peers, and mentors. This feedback can provide insights into areas of improvement and help you refine your skills and strategies. Additionally, finding a mentor can be invaluable. A mentor who has navigated similar paths can offer guidance, advice, and support.

5. Cultivating Soft Skills

While technical skills are important, soft skills like communication, leadership, problem-solving, and emotional intelligence are equally crucial. These skills enhance your ability to work effectively in teams, lead projects, and navigate workplace challenges. Continuously work on developing these skills through practice and training.

6. Embracing Adaptability and Flexibility

The ability to adapt and be flexible is key in today's dynamic work environment. Be open to new challenges and willing to step out of your comfort zone. This might mean taking on new roles, adapting to new technologies, or even changing career paths when necessary.

7. Focusing on Personal Branding

Developing a personal brand can set you apart in the job market. This involves building a reputation for your unique skills and qualities. Be active on professional social media platforms, contribute to industry blogs, or speak at events. This visibility can make you a sought-after professional in your field.

8. Prioritizing Work-Life Balance

Long-term career success is not just about professional achievements; it's also about maintaining a healthy work-life balance. This includes setting boundaries, managing stress, and making time for personal interests and relationships. A well-balanced life can lead to increased productivity and job satisfaction.

9. Being Proactive in Career Management

Finally, take charge of your career path. Don't wait for opportunities to come to you; seek them out. This could mean initiating conversations about career development with your employer, applying for new positions or projects, or even starting your own venture.

Conclusion

Long-term career growth requires a multifaceted approach. It's about setting clear goals, continuously developing skills, building networks, seeking feedback, cultivating soft skills, being adaptable, focusing on personal branding, maintaining work-life balance, and being proactive in your career management. By integrating these strategies into your professional life, you can build a career that is not only successful but also rewarding and fulfilling. In the next chapters, we will explore each of these strategies in detail, providing you with practical tools and insights to apply them effectively in your own career journey.

Chapter 4: The Art of Job Hunting

Traditional vs. Modern Job Search Techniques

In the realm of job hunting, the contrast between traditional and modern techniques is stark, yet both hold value in today's job market. Understanding the nuances of each approach can greatly enhance your job search strategy. Let's delve into the intricacies of these methods, highlighting how they differ and how they can be effectively utilized in your quest for employment.

Traditional Job Search Techniques

Traditional job search methods have been the backbone of employment hunting for decades. These methods are often characterized by a more direct and personal approach.

1. **Newspaper Classifieds and Job Listings**: Once the primary source for job openings, newspaper classifieds are less prevalent now but can still be useful, particularly for local or niche positions.

2. **Walk-In Applications**: This method involves visiting a business in person to inquire about

job openings or submit a resume. While less common now, it's still effective in certain industries like hospitality or retail.

3. **Employment Agencies**: These agencies assist job seekers in finding employment, typically in specific sectors. They often have connections with employers and can provide personalized support.

4. **Networking**: Networking has always been a cornerstone of the job search process. This involves using personal and professional contacts to discover job opportunities.

5. **Direct Mail Campaigns**: Sending targeted resumes and cover letters to selected companies, regardless of whether they have advertised a job opening, can sometimes unearth unadvertised opportunities.

Modern Job Search Techniques

The advent of the digital age has transformed job searching, introducing new methods that leverage technology to enhance the process.

1. **Online Job Boards and Career Websites**: Platforms like LinkedIn, Indeed, and Monster have become primary sources for job listings, offering a vast array of opportunities across various fields and locations.

2. **Social Media Networking**: Utilizing social media platforms, especially LinkedIn, for networking and job searching is increasingly effective. This involves not only connecting with potential employers but also engaging in industry groups and discussions.

3. **Company Websites**: Many companies post job openings on their websites. Regularly checking the careers section of companies you're interested in can be a proactive way to find opportunities.

4. **Email Alerts and Job Search Apps**: Setting up job alerts on various employment websites can provide immediate notifications of relevant job openings. Additionally, job search apps can offer a convenient way to search for jobs on the go.

5. **Virtual Career Fairs and Networking Events**: These online events provide opportunities to connect with employers and learn about job openings from the comfort of your home.

Combining Traditional and Modern Methods

The most effective job search strategy often involves a combination of both traditional and modern techniques. For example, while you may apply for a job online, following up with a phone call or a personal visit (if appropriate) can help you stand out. Similarly, leveraging your network for referrals can complement your online applications.

Adapting to Industry Norms

It's important to note that the effectiveness of these methods can vary by industry. For instance, creative fields may rely more heavily on online portfolios and social media presence, while more traditional sectors might value direct applications and personal connections.

Conclusion

In summary, both traditional and modern job search techniques have their place in the contemporary employment landscape. An effective job search strategy in today's world is not about choosing one over the other but understanding how to use each method to your advantage. By combining the personal touch of traditional methods with the reach and efficiency of modern techniques, you can create a comprehensive approach to your job hunt. In the following chapters, we will explore how to effectively implement these strategies, tailoring your approach to fit your industry, career goals, and personal style.

Leveraging Digital Tools and Social Networks

In the contemporary era, the significance of **leveraging digital tools and social networks** in the context of job searching and career development cannot be overstated. These modern platforms offer unprecedented opportunities for networking, brand building, and accessing job markets. Let's explore the various aspects of these digital resources and how they can be effectively utilized to enhance your career prospects.

Understanding the Digital Landscape

The digital world offers a plethora of tools and platforms that can be harnessed for job searching and professional networking. These include professional networking sites like LinkedIn, job search engines like Indeed and Glassdoor, and even broader social networks like Twitter and Facebook. Each platform has its unique features and best practices.

Maximizing LinkedIn for Professional Networking

LinkedIn is arguably the most significant professional networking site. It's not just a place to post your resume; it's a platform for connecting with industry leaders, joining professional groups, and engaging with content relevant to your field. Here are some ways to maximize its potential:

- **Optimize Your Profile**: Ensure your LinkedIn profile is complete and up-to-date, highlighting your skills, experiences, and achievements. Use a professional photo and craft a compelling summary that reflects your career aspirations.

- **Networking**: Connect with colleagues, industry experts, and alumni. Regularly engage with their content through likes, comments, and shares.

- **Content Creation**: Share your insights, write articles, or post updates related to your field to demonstrate your expertise and opinions.

- **Job Searching**: Utilize LinkedIn's job search functionality. Apply for posted jobs and enable job alerts tailored to your career interests.

Utilizing Job Search Engines Effectively

Websites like Indeed, Monster, and Glassdoor are powerful tools for finding job openings. They aggregate listings from various sources, providing a comprehensive view of the job market.

- **Resume and Cover Letter**: Upload your resume and customize your cover letter for each application to increase your chances of standing out.

- **Search Filters**: Use specific keywords and filters to refine your job search based on location, industry, and job type.

- **Company Research**: These platforms often provide insights into company cultures, salaries, and reviews, which can be invaluable in your job search process.

Engaging on Broader Social Networks

Platforms like Twitter, Facebook, and Instagram can also be leveraged for professional purposes.

- **Follow Industry Leaders and Companies**: Stay informed about industry trends and job openings by following relevant accounts.

- **Join Groups and Communities**: Participate in discussions and networking opportunities in groups related to your field.

- **Share Content**: Post content that reflects your professional interests and expertise.

Building a Personal Brand Online

Your online presence can significantly impact your career prospects. A strong personal brand makes you more attractive to potential employers.

- **Consistent Online Persona**: Ensure your online profiles across various platforms are consistent and reflect your professional self.

- **Blog or Personal Website**: Consider starting a blog or a personal website to showcase your portfolio, share your thoughts on industry trends, or highlight your skills.

Staying Informed Through Digital Media

Subscribe to industry blogs, podcasts, and newsletters to stay updated on the latest trends and opportunities in your field.

Data Privacy and Online Conduct

Be mindful of your digital footprint. Maintain professionalism in all your online interactions and be aware of the privacy settings on various platforms.

Conclusion

The digital realm offers a multitude of tools and platforms that can be strategically utilized for career advancement. From networking on LinkedIn to searching for jobs on dedicated platforms, and building a personal brand across social networks, these digital tools enable you to access global opportunities and connect with professionals worldwide. In the upcoming chapters, we will dive deeper into specific strategies for each platform, ensuring you are equipped to fully leverage the power of digital tools and social networks in your career journey.

Chapter 5: Thriving in a New Job Environment

Integrating into Diverse Work Cultures

In today's globalized world, the ability to integrate into diverse work cultures is not just an asset; it's a necessity. Workplaces are increasingly becoming melting pots of various cultures, ethnicities, and backgrounds. This diversity brings a wealth of perspectives and ideas, but it also presents challenges in terms of integration and understanding. Let's delve into strategies for successfully navigating and embracing diverse work cultures.

Understanding Cultural Diversity

The first step towards integrating into diverse work cultures is understanding what cultural diversity entails. It's not just about national or ethnic differences. It encompasses a range of elements including language, religion, gender, age, socio-economic background, and more. Each of these aspects contributes to how individuals perceive the world and interact within it.

Active Listening and Observation

Upon entering a new workplace, spend time actively listening and observing. This helps in understanding the dynamics of the workplace, the informal norms, and the communication styles. Pay attention to how decisions are made, how conflicts are resolved, and how meetings are conducted. Observation is key to understanding the subtle nuances of a new work culture.

Cultural Sensitivity and Awareness

Develop cultural sensitivity by educating yourself about the different cultures represented in your workplace. This could involve formal training or self-directed learning. Understanding basic cultural norms, communication styles, and taboos can prevent misunderstandings and build mutual respect.

Effective Communication

Communication styles vary significantly across cultures. Some cultures may value directness, while others may prefer more indirect ways of expressing disagreement. Being aware of these differences and adapting your communication style can greatly enhance your ability to work effectively in a diverse environment.

Building Relationships

Take the initiative to build relationships with your colleagues. This might involve participating in social activities, offering help when needed, or simply engaging in regular, informal conversations. Building trust and rapport is essential in any workplace, but particularly so in diverse environments where misunderstandings can arise more easily.

Seeking Feedback

Be open to feedback and be proactive in seeking it. Understanding how your actions and words are perceived by colleagues from different cultural backgrounds can provide valuable insights and help in adjusting your behavior.

Flexibility and Adaptability

Being flexible and adaptable is crucial. This means being open to different ways of doing things and being willing to adjust your work style and expectations. Remember that your way of working is not the only way, nor necessarily the best way in a given context.

Advocating for Inclusivity

Take an active role in advocating for an inclusive workplace. This could involve participating in or setting up committees focused on diversity, suggesting training sessions, or simply being a role model for inclusive behavior.

Dealing with Challenges

If you face challenges or misunderstandings due to cultural differences, address them respectfully and directly. Seek to understand the other person's perspective and explain your own clearly and calmly.

Lifelong Learning

Finally, view cultural integration as a lifelong learning process. The more you interact with different cultures, the more you will learn and grow. This journey is not just about being effective in diverse workplaces; it's about becoming a more empathic and well-rounded individual.

Conclusion

Integrating into diverse work cultures requires effort, sensitivity, and a willingness to learn and adapt. By understanding and embracing cultural differences, you can unlock the full potential of a diverse workplace, leading to richer collaborations, more creative ideas, and a more fulfilling professional experience. In the next chapters, we will explore specific case studies and strategies that highlight successful integration into various work cultures, providing you with practical examples and lessons learned.

Building Resilience and Emotional Intelligence

In the constantly evolving landscape of the modern workplace, two critical skills stand out for their importance in navigating both success and setbacks: **resilience** and **emotional intelligence**. As we explore these concepts, it's essential to understand not only what they are but also how to actively develop and harness them in your professional life.

Understanding Resilience in the Workplace

Resilience refers to the ability to adapt well in the face of adversity, trauma, tragedy, threats, or significant sources of stress. In the context of a career, it means bouncing back from challenges and disappointments while maintaining a stable mental and emotional state.

1. **Identifying Sources of Resilience**: Understand that resilience stems from various sources, including personal values, your support system, and your own mindset. Recognizing these sources is the first step in harnessing your resilience.

2. **Cultivating a Growth Mindset**: Embrace challenges as opportunities for learning and growth. A growth mindset, as opposed to a fixed mindset, is essential for resilience. It's about believing that skills and intelligence can be developed over time.

3. **Developing Problem-Solving Skills**: Resilient individuals approach problems with a sense of confidence and proactivity. Enhance your problem-solving skills by facing challenges head-on and seeking innovative solutions.

4. **Embracing Change**: Change is inevitable in any career. Resilient individuals adapt to changing circumstances and view them as opportunities rather than insurmountable obstacles.

5. **Practicing Self-Care**: Prioritizing your physical and mental health is crucial. Self-care practices like regular exercise, adequate sleep, and mindfulness can bolster your resilience.

Fostering Emotional Intelligence (EI)

Emotional intelligence is the ability to understand and manage your own emotions and those of others. In the workplace, EI is invaluable for leadership, teamwork, and overall job performance.

1. **Self-Awareness**: This is the foundation of EI. It involves understanding your emotions, strengths, weaknesses, and drives. Keep a journal, reflect on your experiences, and seek feedback to enhance self-awareness.

2. **Self-Regulation**: This involves controlling or redirecting disruptive emotions and adapting to changing circumstances. Practice patience, think before acting, and express your emotions appropriately.

3. **Motivation**: High EI individuals are motivated by things beyond external rewards like fame, money, or recognition. They are passionate about their work, pursue goals with energy and persistence, and are driven by an inner ambition.

4. **Empathy**: The ability to understand the emotional makeup of other people. It's about treating everyone with respect, being good at listening, and genuinely caring about others' well-being.

5. **Social Skills**: Being able to build rapport and maintain relationships is a crucial aspect of EI. It's about effective communication, conflict management, and being a team player.

Integrating Resilience and EI in Your Career

- **Continuous Learning**: Always be open to learning, whether it's from experiences, successes, failures, or other people. This openness is a key component of both resilience and EI.

- **Networking and Mentorship**: Cultivate a strong professional network and seek mentors who exemplify high resilience and EI. Learn from their experiences and insights.

- **Feedback and Reflection**: Regularly seek feedback on your performance and reflect on it. Use this feedback to improve your resilience and emotional intelligence.

- **Practicing Mindfulness**: Mindfulness techniques can enhance both resilience and EI by helping you stay centered and aware in the face of work-related stress.

- **Setting Boundaries**: Understand your limits and learn to say no. Setting healthy boundaries is vital for maintaining resilience and emotional balance.

Conclusion

Building resilience and emotional intelligence is not an overnight task but a continuous journey. It involves a deep understanding of self, a commitment to personal growth, and the ability to navigate the complexities of interpersonal dynamics in the workplace. As you progress in your career, these skills will not only help you withstand challenges but also thrive amidst them, paving the way for a fulfilling and sustainable career. In the following chapters, we will explore practical exercises and case studies that illustrate the development and application of resilience and emotional intelligence in various professional scenarios.

Chapter 6: Navigating Career Transitions

When and How to Seek New Opportunities

In the dynamic and ever-changing world of work, understanding when and how to seek new opportunities is a vital skill. It's about recognizing the right moment to make a move and knowing the most effective strategies to do so. This pursuit is not merely about changing jobs; it's about strategically advancing your career and ensuring continual growth and fulfillment.

Recognizing the Right Time to Seek New Opportunities

1. **Lack of Growth or Learning**: If your current role no longer challenges you or offers opportunities for growth, it may be time to look elsewhere. Continuous learning and development are key to maintaining an evergreen career.

2. **Misalignment with Personal Goals or Values**: When your job is no longer aligned with your personal goals, values, or life

situation, consider seeking opportunities that offer a better fit.

3. **Changes in the Industry or Company**: Significant changes such as mergers, acquisitions, or shifts in industry trends can affect your job's stability and future prospects. These changes might prompt a search for new opportunities.

4. **Desire for a New Challenge**: Sometimes, the motivation to move comes from a desire to tackle new challenges, explore different industries, or step into roles with greater responsibilities.

How to Seek New Opportunities Effectively

1. **Self-Assessment**: Begin with a thorough self-assessment. Understand your strengths, weaknesses, and what you are looking for in your next role. Consider factors like job content, company culture, location, and work-life balance.

2. **Update Your Resume and Online Profiles**: Ensure your resume is updated, highlighting recent achievements and skills. Your LinkedIn profile and other professional social media should also be current and reflect your career aspirations.

3. **Network Strategically**: Networking is key in uncovering new opportunities. Attend industry events, join professional groups, and reconnect with former colleagues. Inform your network that you're open to new opportunities.

4. **Utilize Job Search Engines and Company Websites**: Regularly browse job search engines and the careers sections of company websites. Set up alerts for job titles or companies you're interested in.

5. **Engage with Recruiters**: Recruiters can be valuable allies in your job search. Reach out to recruitment agencies that specialize in your field or desired industry.

6. **Leverage Social Media**: Platforms like LinkedIn, Twitter, and even Instagram can be used to connect with industry leaders, follow companies, and learn about job openings.

7. **Customize Applications**: Tailor your resume and cover letter for each application. Highlight specific skills and experiences that align with the job description.

8. **Prepare for Interviews**: Brush up on interview skills. Be ready to discuss your experiences, accomplishments, and how they align with the potential new role.

9. **Consider Company Culture**: Research company cultures to find a good fit. Use resources like Glassdoor to get insights into the companies you are interested in.

10. **Evaluate Job Offers Thoroughly**: When you receive job offers, evaluate them carefully. Consider all aspects, including salary, benefits, career growth opportunities, company culture, and the role itself.

Conclusion

Seeking new opportunities is a proactive step in managing your career. It's about making deliberate choices based on a clear understanding of your career goals and the market landscape. Remember, each move should be a strategic step toward your long-term career objectives. In the next chapters, we will explore case studies that illustrate successful transitions and provide insights into making informed career decisions.

Making the Most of Career Breaks and Shifts

Career breaks and shifts are often viewed with apprehension, but in reality, they can be powerful catalysts for professional growth and personal development. In the evolving landscape of work, where linear career paths are becoming less common, understanding how to navigate and maximize these periods is crucial. Let's explore the strategies and mindsets needed to turn career breaks and shifts into opportunities for enrichment and advancement.

Embracing Career Breaks

Career breaks, whether planned or unplanned, can occur for various reasons: pursuing further education, personal health issues, family commitments, travel, or simply taking time to reassess career goals. Here's how to make the most of these periods:

1. **Self-Reflection**: Use this time for introspection. Assess your career progress, clarify your goals, and consider what you want from your next professional chapter.

2. **Skill Development**: Career breaks are an excellent opportunity to upgrade skills or learn new ones. Online courses, workshops, or even self-taught skills can enhance your resume.

3. **Networking**: Maintain and expand your professional network. Attend industry events,

join online forums, or schedule informational interviews to stay connected.

4. **Personal Projects**: Engage in projects that you're passionate about. Whether it's a freelance gig, a creative pursuit, or volunteer work, these activities can lead to new career insights and opportunities.

5. **Wellness and Balance**: Focus on your well-being. A career break can be a time to rejuvenate and ensure that you return to the workforce with renewed energy and perspective.

Navigating Career Shifts

A career shift, whether a change in job function, industry, or a complete career transformation, requires careful navigation. Here's how to approach these shifts:

1. **Transferable Skills**: Identify skills that can transfer to your new role or industry. Emphasize these in your applications and interviews to demonstrate your suitability.

2. **Research and Preparation**: Thoroughly research the new field. Understand the industry dynamics, required skill sets, and key players. This knowledge will guide your

transition and conversations with potential employers.

3. **Start Small**: If a direct transition seems challenging, consider interim steps. This could include roles that bridge your current experience with your desired field.

4. **Seek Support**: Connect with professionals already in the field. Seek mentors who can provide guidance and insight into your desired career path.

5. **Rebrand Yourself**: Update your resume, LinkedIn profile, and other professional materials to reflect your new career direction. Highlight your relevant skills and experiences that align with your new path.

Overcoming Challenges

Career breaks and shifts can come with challenges such as skill gaps, industry changes, or even biases against employment gaps. Here's how to address these challenges:

1. **Proactive Explanation**: Be prepared to explain your career break or shift in a positive and proactive manner. Focus on what you learned during that time and how it's relevant to your career goals.

2. **Stay Informed**: Even during a break, stay updated on industry trends and changes. This will make your transition back into the workforce smoother.

3. **Flexibility in Job Search**: Be open to different types of roles, including part-time, freelance, or contract work, as they can be stepping stones to full-time positions.

4. **Building Confidence**: Career changes can be daunting. Build confidence through small successes, continuous learning, and positive self-talk.

Conclusion

Career breaks and shifts, when navigated thoughtfully, can be transformative. They offer a chance to reassess, learn, and grow in ways that continuous employment may not always allow. By embracing these periods with an open mind and strategic approach, you can emerge with new skills, clearer goals, and renewed vigor, ready to embark on the next phase of your evergreen employment journey. In the next chapters, we will explore real-life stories of individuals who have successfully navigated career breaks and shifts, offering insights and inspiration for your own career path.

Chapter 7: The Future of Work

Emerging Trends and Predictions

In an era marked by rapid technological advancements and shifting economic tides, staying abreast of emerging trends and predictions in employment is paramount. As we stand at the cusp of new developments in the world of work, it's crucial to anticipate and prepare for the changes that lie ahead. Let's delve into some of the key trends shaping the future of employment and how they might influence your career trajectory.

1. The Rise of Remote and Flexible Work

The digital age has ushered in an era where remote work is becoming increasingly feasible and popular. The COVID-19 pandemic accelerated this trend, demonstrating that many jobs can be done effectively outside of traditional office settings.

- **Increased Flexibility**: Employers are recognizing the benefits of flexible work arrangements, including increased productivity and employee satisfaction.

- **Global Talent Pool**: Remote work opens up opportunities for employers to tap into a global talent pool and for employees to seek jobs worldwide.

- **Technological Advancements**: The continued development of collaborative tools and technologies will further facilitate remote work.

2. The Gig Economy and Freelancing

The gig economy, characterized by short-term contracts or freelance work as opposed to permanent jobs, is on the rise. This trend offers flexibility and autonomy but also brings challenges regarding job security and benefits.

- **Diversified Income Sources**: Professionals are increasingly looking at freelancing and contract work as viable options for diversifying their income sources.

- **Skill Specialization**: In the gig economy, there is a growing emphasis on specialized skills and the ability to quickly adapt to different projects and working conditions.

3. Artificial Intelligence and Automation

AI and automation are transforming the job market, automating certain tasks, and creating new types of jobs.

- **Job Displacement and Creation**: While some jobs may be automated, new jobs will be created, especially those requiring complex problem-solving and creative thinking.

- **Upskilling and Reskilling**: Continuous learning to adapt to new technologies will be crucial for staying relevant in the job market.

4. Focus on Mental Health and Well-being

There's an increasing recognition of the importance of mental health and well-being in the workplace.

- **Work-Life Balance**: Employers are implementing policies to promote work-life balance, understanding its impact on productivity and employee retention.

- **Employee Support Programs**: More companies are offering support programs addressing mental health, including counseling services and wellness initiatives.

5. Sustainability and Corporate Responsibility

Sustainability and corporate social responsibility are becoming critical factors in organizational strategies and consumer preferences.

- **Green Jobs**: There will be a surge in 'green jobs' as companies invest in sustainable practices and technologies.

- **Ethical Employment Practices**: Organizations focusing on ethical practices and sustainability will attract top talent who prioritize these values.

6. Lifelong Learning and Continuous Education

The need for continuous education and upskilling will become more pronounced as the job market evolves.

- **Online Learning Platforms**: Access to online courses and training will enable professionals to continuously upgrade their skills.

- **Micro-Credentials**: There will be a rise in micro-credentials and certifications allowing professionals to demonstrate their expertise in specific areas.

7. Changing Demographics and Inclusivity

The workforce is becoming more diverse, and inclusivity is becoming a key focus area.

- **Age Diversity**: With people working longer, there will be more age diversity in the workplace.

- **Inclusivity Policies**: Companies are increasingly adopting inclusivity policies, recognizing the value of a diverse workforce.

Conclusion

As we navigate through these emerging trends, it's clear that the future of work is both exciting and challenging. Staying informed and adaptable, continuously upskilling, and being open to new ways of working will be essential strategies for success. The ability to anticipate and adapt to these changes will define the careers of tomorrow. In the following chapters, we will delve deeper into each of these trends, providing insights and strategies to effectively navigate and capitalize on them, ensuring that your career remains resilient and vibrant in the face of change.

Preparing for Tomorrow's Job Landscape

As we stand on the threshold of significant shifts in the job market, preparing for tomorrow's landscape is imperative. The future of work is not just a distant concept; it's a rapidly unfolding reality shaped by technological advancements, cultural shifts, and economic changes. Let's explore how you can equip yourself to thrive in this dynamic environment.

Understanding the Future Work Environment

1. **Technological Integration**: The future job landscape will be increasingly intertwined with technology. Familiarity with artificial intelligence, machine learning, and data analytics, regardless of your field, will be advantageous.

2. **Remote and Hybrid Work Models**: Post-pandemic, the adoption of remote and hybrid work models is expected to continue. Adapting to these models requires not only technological proficiency but also self-discipline and effective virtual communication skills.

3. **The Gig Economy**: With the rise of project-based and freelance work, adaptability to the gig economy is crucial. This includes

managing multiple projects, continuous learning, and personal branding.

Skills for the Future

1. **Technical Skills**: Stay abreast of the technical skills required in your industry. Continuous learning through online courses, workshops, and certifications will be key.

2. **Soft Skills**: Skills such as critical thinking, creativity, problem-solving, adaptability, and emotional intelligence will become even more valuable. These skills enable you to navigate complex environments and collaborate effectively.

3. **Digital Literacy**: Proficiency in digital tools and platforms is already essential and will only grow in importance. Understanding digital workflows, cybersecurity basics, and digital collaboration tools is fundamental.

Lifelong Learning and Up-skilling

1. **Continuous Education**: The concept of education as a lifelong endeavor is central to thriving in the future job market. This includes formal education and informal learning opportunities.

2. **Micro-credentials**: Short, focused learning modules or micro-credentials will become increasingly popular for acquiring specific skills quickly and efficiently.

Adapting to New Work Cultures

1. **Cultural Agility**: As workplaces become more diverse and global, cultural agility – the ability to quickly, comfortably, and effectively work in different cultures and with people from different cultures – will be crucial.

2. **Inclusivity and Collaboration**: Skills in fostering an inclusive environment and collaborating across diverse teams will be critical.

Personal Branding and Online Presence

1. **Building a Personal Brand**: In a digital-first world, how you present yourself online is critical. Consistently curate your online presence to reflect your professional identity and values.

2. **Networking**: Leverage social media platforms for networking. Engaging with industry leaders, participating in online forums, and building a professional network online will open doors to new opportunities.

Mental Resilience and Flexibility

1. **Emotional Well-being**: Prioritize your mental health. The ability to cope with stress, uncertainty, and rapid changes is as important as any technical skill.

2. **Flexibility and Adaptability**: Be open to changing career paths, learning new skills, and embracing new ways of working.

Conclusion

The future job landscape will be characterized by constant change, requiring a proactive approach to career development. Embracing continuous learning, honing both technical and soft skills, adapting to new work environments, and maintaining a robust online presence are all strategies that will equip you to not just survive but thrive in the future of work. In the upcoming chapters, we will delve deeper into how you can develop each of these areas, complete with actionable steps and real-life examples, to ensure that your career remains resilient, adaptable, and fulfilling, no matter what the future holds.

Conclusion: Your Evergreen Employment Journey

Synthesizing Learning into Action

In the intricate dance of career progression, the ability to synthesize learning into action is what sets apart truly successful professionals. It's one thing to absorb information or develop new skills; it's quite another to apply this knowledge effectively in the workplace. This crucial step transforms theoretical understanding into tangible results, leading to career advancement and personal fulfillment. Let's explore how you can effectively bridge the gap between learning and doing.

1. Translating Skills into Practical Applications

- **Identify Opportunities**: Look for opportunities in your current role where new skills can be applied. This could mean volunteering for new projects, suggesting improvements, or implementing new processes.

- **Set Clear Goals**: Define what you want to achieve by applying new skills. Setting specific, measurable goals gives you a target to aim for and a way to track your progress.

- **Create a Plan**: Develop a step-by-step plan for how you will apply your new skills. This could involve setting timelines, identifying resources, or seeking support from colleagues or mentors.

2. Building a Learning-Focused Mindset

- **Embrace Continuous Improvement**: Cultivate a mindset that views every task as an opportunity to learn and improve. This attitude will keep you open to applying new knowledge and adapting to feedback.

- **Reflect on Learning**: Regular reflection is key. After applying a new skill, take the time to reflect on what worked, what didn't, and how you can improve next time.

3. Leveraging Feedback and Reflection

- **Seek Feedback**: Ask for feedback from peers, supervisors, or mentors. Understanding how others perceive your application of new skills can provide valuable insights.

- **Reflect on Outcomes**: Analyze the outcomes of applying new knowledge. Did it meet your goals? What unexpected challenges arose? How can you adapt your approach in the future?

4. Integrating Learning with Team Collaboration

- **Share Knowledge**: Share your learnings with your team. Teaching others can reinforce your own understanding and benefit your entire team.

- **Collaborate on Application**: Look for ways to collaborate with colleagues when applying new skills. Team projects can be excellent opportunities to put learning into practice.

5. Staying Adaptable to Change

- **Embrace Experimentation**: Be open to experimenting with different ways to apply your skills. Not every attempt will be successful, but each will provide valuable learning experiences.

- **Adapt to Feedback and Results**: Use feedback and the results of your efforts to refine your approach. Adaptability is key in successfully applying new knowledge.

6. Documenting and Reflecting on Your Journey

- **Keep a Learning Journal**: Documenting your journey of applying new skills can be incredibly insightful. Note what you've tried, the results, and your reflections on the process.

- **Celebrate Successes**: Acknowledge and celebrate when you successfully apply new skills. This not only boosts confidence but also motivates you to continue learning and applying new knowledge.

7. Applying Learning Beyond Your Current Role

- **Consider Long-Term Career Goals**: Think about how the skills you're learning and applying align with your long-term career goals. Are there additional areas you need to focus on?

- **Be Open to New Opportunities**: Sometimes, the best way to apply new learning is in a new role or environment. Be open to seeking new opportunities where your enhanced skill set will be valued.

Conclusion

In conclusion, synthesizing learning into action is a dynamic and ongoing process. It requires setting clear goals, building a learning-focused mindset, leveraging feedback, collaborating with others, staying adaptable, and constantly reflecting on your progress. By mastering this process, you transform yourself into a lifelong learner and an action-oriented professional, fully prepared to meet the challenges of an ever-changing job landscape. In the next and final chapter, we will explore how to embrace a lifetime of career evolution, ensuring that your professional journey is not just successful but also personally rewarding and aligned with your evergreen employment goals.

Embracing a Lifetime of Career Evolution

In the vast and varied expanse of the professional world, embracing a lifetime of career evolution is not just a strategy; it's a necessity for enduring success and fulfillment. As we traverse through different phases of our working lives, the concept of career evolution becomes integral to our narrative. This evolution is not merely a sequence of job changes or promotions; it's a continuous journey of growth, learning, and adaptation. Let's explore the facets of this journey and how to navigate it with purpose and agility.

Understanding the Nature of Career Evolution

- **Dynamic Career Paths**: Gone are the days of linear career paths. Today's professional trajectories are more akin to a lattice, with moves in various directions, including lateral shifts, upward movements, and sometimes even steps back to gain new skills or experiences.

- **Continuous Learning**: The heart of career evolution lies in perpetual learning. Staying relevant in your field or pivoting to a new one requires an ongoing commitment to acquiring new knowledge and skills.

Strategies for Nurturing Career Evolution

1. **Proactive Career Planning**: Regularly assess your career goals and align them with your personal values and market trends. This proactive planning helps in making informed decisions about your career trajectory.

2. **Seeking Diverse Experiences**: Embrace opportunities to work in different roles, industries, or even geographic locations. These experiences not only enhance your

resume but also broaden your perspective and skill set.

3. **Networking and Mentorship**: Cultivate a diverse network and seek mentors who can offer guidance and insight. The wisdom gleaned from others' experiences can be invaluable in navigating your career path.

4. **Personal Branding**: Develop and maintain a strong personal brand. Your brand should reflect your professional identity, strengths, and the unique value you bring to the table.

5. **Embracing Change and Adaptability**: Be open to change and willing to adapt. The ability to pivot in response to industry shifts or personal circumstances is crucial in maintaining a dynamic and relevant career.

Balancing Ambition with Well-being

- **Mindful Career Moves**: While ambition is a key driver of career evolution, it's important to balance it with personal well-being. Ensure that your career decisions do not compromise your health, relationships, or overall quality of life.

- **Setting Boundaries**: Learn to set healthy boundaries to prevent burnout. Knowing when to say no or when to take a break is as important as seizing opportunities.

Leveraging Failures and Setbacks

- **Learning from Failures**: View failures and setbacks as learning opportunities. Reflect on what went wrong, what you could have done differently, and how you can avoid similar pitfalls in the future.

- **Resilience**: Develop resilience to bounce back from disappointments. Resilience is built through facing challenges and learning to navigate them effectively.

Preparing for the Unpredictable

- **Flexibility in Career Goals**: While it's important to have career goals, be flexible in how you achieve them. The unpredictable nature of the job market might require you to adjust your path or timelines.

- **Staying Informed**: Keep abreast of emerging trends and predictions in your field. This knowledge will help you anticipate changes and make strategic career moves.

Conclusion

Embracing a lifetime of career evolution is about understanding that your professional journey is unique and ever-changing. It involves being proactive, adaptable, resilient, and open to learning. It's about making strategic choices, learning from experiences, and balancing professional aspirations with personal well-being. As you continue on your evergreen employment journey, remember that each step, each decision, and each transition is a part of a larger narrative - one that you are continuously crafting with your choices, actions, and perspectives. In the appendices, you'll find additional resources, case studies, and success stories that will provide further insights into navigating your unique career path.

Appendices

Case Studies and Success Stories

In my journey exploring the ever-changing world of employment, I have encountered numerous inspiring case studies and success stories. These narratives not only demonstrate the principles of evergreen employment but also offer practical insights and encouragement for anyone navigating their own career path. Let's delve into a few of these transformative stories, highlighting the key lessons and strategies that contributed to their success.

1. The Pivot from Traditional Industry to Tech Start-up

- **Background**: Sarah, a mid-level manager in a traditional manufacturing company, faced a stagnant career path. With the industry declining, she decided to pivot to a technology start-up.

- **Strategy**: Sarah leveraged her transferable skills, emphasizing her leadership abilities and project management experience. She also enrolled in online courses to boost her understanding of the tech sector.

- **Outcome**: Sarah successfully transitioned to a project manager role at a promising tech start-up, bringing a fresh perspective from her manufacturing background. Her adaptability and eagerness to learn new skills played a crucial role in her successful career shift.

2. The Return to the Workforce After a Career Break

- **Background**: Mark took a five-year career break to care for his young children. Returning to the job market, he faced challenges due to his employment gap.

- **Strategy**: Mark focused on updating his skills and leveraging his network. He undertook part-time consulting projects to build a recent track record of work and attended industry networking events.

- **Outcome**: By demonstrating his updated skillset and staying connected to the industry, Mark secured a role that valued his life experience and new perspectives.

3. Embracing Remote Work for Greater Work-Life Balance

- **Background**: Emily, a software developer, sought better work-life balance after the birth of her first child. She explored remote work opportunities to achieve this goal.

- **Strategy**: Emily focused on companies known for their flexible work cultures. She highlighted her ability to work independently and her experience with remote collaboration tools during her job search.

- **Outcome**: Emily landed a remote position with a tech company that offered flexibility and a supportive work environment, allowing her to balance her professional and personal life effectively.

4. The Continuous Learner Who Became an Industry Expert

- **Background**: Alex, starting as a junior marketing assistant, had a passion for digital marketing but limited formal education in the field.

- **Strategy**: Alex embraced continuous learning, completing online courses and certifications in digital marketing. He also actively contributed to marketing forums and blogs, sharing his insights and learning from peers.

- **Outcome**: Over time, Alex's dedication to learning and sharing knowledge led to him becoming a recognized expert in digital marketing. He advanced to a senior role and was invited to speak at industry conferences.

5. The Freelancer's Journey to Entrepreneurship

- **Background**: Mia began her career as a freelance graphic designer, enjoying the flexibility but facing income instability.

- **Strategy**: Mia gradually built a robust client base and hired other freelancers to assist with projects. She focused on building her personal brand and networking extensively.

- **Outcome**: Mia eventually founded her own design agency, leveraging her freelance experience and client relationships. Her agency now thrives, offering her both financial stability and creative satisfaction.

Conclusion

These stories underscore the power of adaptability, continuous learning, networking, personal branding, and resilience. Each individual faced unique challenges but shared a common commitment to evolving their careers in response to changing circumstances and opportunities. As we navigate our own professional journeys, these narratives serve as both inspiration and a roadmap, reminding us that with the right strategies and mindset, we can achieve our career aspirations, no matter how the job landscape evolves.

Additional Resources and Reading

In the pursuit of an evergreen career, the value of continuous learning and resourcefulness cannot be overstated. I have come across an array of invaluable resources and readings that have shaped my understanding of the employment landscape. These resources are instrumental for anyone looking to deepen their knowledge and skills in navigating the job market and career development. Let's explore some of these essential resources that can further enrich your professional journey.

Books and Publications

1. **"What Color Is Your Parachute?" by Richard N. Bolles**: A timeless classic, this book offers practical advice for job-hunters and career-changers. It's updated annually to reflect the latest job market trends.

2. **"Drive: The Surprising Truth About What Motivates Us" by Daniel H. Pink**: This book explores the intricacies of motivation in the

workplace and provides insights into how to find personal satisfaction in our careers.

3. **"Lean In: Women, Work, and the Will to Lead" by Sheryl Sandberg**: Focusing on issues of leadership and gender in the workplace, Sandberg's book is a call to action for women to pursue their career goals fearlessly.

4. **"The 7 Habits of Highly Effective People" by Stephen R. Covey**: Covey's book is a guide for personal and professional effectiveness, offering a principle-centered approach to solving personal and professional problems.

5. **Harvard Business Review**: A leading resource offering a wealth of articles, case studies, and reports on the latest trends in business and management.

Online Courses and Platforms

1. **Coursera & Udemy**: These platforms offer courses on a wide range of subjects, from technical skills like data analysis and coding to soft skills like leadership and communication.

2. **LinkedIn Learning**: Provides a vast array of courses tailored towards career development and skill enhancement in various industries.

Podcasts and Video Channels

1. **"How I Built This" with Guy Raz**: A podcast that delves into the stories behind some of the world's best-known companies and their creators.

2. **"WorkLife" with Adam Grant**: Adam Grant explores the science of work and how to make work not suck.

3. **TED Talks**: Offers a range of insightful talks from experts on topics including career development, innovation, and motivation.

Professional Networks and Forums

1. **LinkedIn**: Beyond a job search tool, LinkedIn offers an opportunity to connect with industry leaders, join professional groups, and engage in meaningful discussions.

2. **Industry-Specific Forums**: Platforms like Stack Overflow for tech professionals or Behance for creatives provide community support and networking opportunities.

Journals and Research Publications

1. **The Journal of Applied Psychology**: Offers in-depth research articles on topics relevant to

employment, career development, and organizational psychology.

2. **McKinsey Quarterly**: Provides insights and analyses on global management trends.

Career Development Centers and Workshops

1. **Local University Career Centers**: Many universities offer career development workshops and counseling services that are open to the public.

2. **Professional Development Workshops**: Organizations like the American Management Association (AMA) offer workshops and seminars on various aspects of career advancement and management skills.

Conclusion

Empowering yourself with knowledge and insights from these varied resources can significantly enhance your career journey. Whether it's through reading insightful books, participating in online courses, engaging in professional networks, or attending workshops, each step you take in absorbing this wealth of knowledge brings you closer to achieving an evergreen career. Remember, in the world of work, your education and development are never complete. There's always more to learn, more to explore, and more ways to grow.

Acknowledgments

As I reflect on the journey of creating "Evergreen Employment, Unveiling Timeless Job Wisdom," I am deeply aware that this endeavor is not a solo achievement but a tapestry woven with the support, insights, and contributions of many remarkable individuals. It is with immense gratitude that I acknowledge those who have been instrumental in this endeavor.

Professional Mentors and Colleagues

- **Johnathan Rivers**: My mentor, whose wisdom in the field of career development has been a guiding light. His invaluable advice and unwavering support have shaped many of the insights in this book.

- **The Team at Bright Future Consulting**: Colleagues who have been a source of inspiration and knowledge. Their experiences and perspectives on the evolving job market have enriched the content of this book significantly.

Industry Experts and Thought Leaders

- **Elizabeth Harmon and Michael Zhou**: Whose pioneering research in the field of employment trends provided a foundation for the chapters on future work dynamics.

- **Sophia Martinez**: A leading voice in digital transformation, whose insights into the digital age of employment were invaluable.

Editorial and Publishing Support

- **Hannah Leigh & The Editorial Team at Apex Publishing**: For their meticulous attention to detail and commitment to maintaining the integrity of the book's vision.

- **Linda Graham at Creative Design Studios**: Whose expertise in design brought visual elegance to this work.

Personal Support System

- **My Family**: For their endless patience, understanding, and encouragement throughout the countless hours dedicated to researching and writing.

- **My Friends**: Who provided much-needed breaks and laughter, reminding me of the world beyond the pages.

Academic and Research Contributors

- **Professors at the London School of Economics**: Whose academic work in labor history informed the historical context discussed in the early chapters.

- **The Research Team at Global Employment Insights**: For providing access to valuable data and trends in the job market.

Community and Reader Feedback

- **Readers of Preliminary Drafts**: Whose feedback was crucial in shaping the final manuscript. Their questions and comments ensured that the book remained relevant and accessible.

- **Online Professional Communities**: Whose discussions and debates on platforms like LinkedIn provided real-time insights into the challenges and triumphs of today's workforce.

Inspiration and Creative Influences

- **The Countless Stories of Career Journeys**: Shared with me over the years by individuals from diverse backgrounds. These stories have been the heartbeat of this book, providing real-life examples of resilience, adaptation, and success.

Final Word of Gratitude

As I conclude this section, my heart is full of gratitude. This book is a culmination of shared knowledge, collaborative effort, and collective wisdom. To all who have been a part of this journey, I extend my deepest thanks. Your contributions have not only enriched this book but have also deeply enriched my personal and professional life. It is my sincere hope that "Evergreen Employment" will serve as a valuable guide and inspiration to all its readers, just as your support has been to me.

About the Author

Morgan E. Blake, the author of "Evergreen Employment, Unveiling Timeless Job Wisdom," stands as a beacon in the realm of employment and career development. Choosing to write under a pseudonym, Blake brings a unique perspective to the complex and ever-evolving world of work. This anonymity serves as a testament to Blake's commitment to delivering objective, uncolored insights, ensuring that the focus remains solely on the invaluable guidance provided to the reader.

Background and Career Journey

- **Educational Foundation**: Blake's foray into the world of employment strategy began with a solid educational background in Human Resource Management and Organizational Psychology, laying the foundation for a deep understanding of the job market dynamics.

- **Professional Experience**: With a career spanning over two decades, Blake has garnered extensive experience in various facets of employment, including recruitment, career coaching, and human resources consulting. This diverse exposure has equipped Blake with a holistic view of the job market.

- **Industry Recognition**: Known for insightful analyses and strategic thinking, Blake has been a sought-after consultant for numerous Fortune 500 companies, start-ups, and non-profit organizations, providing tailored advice on workforce development and career planning.

Philosophy and Approach

- **Focus on Evergreen Principles**: Blake's approach to career development emphasizes the importance of 'evergreen' principles - timeless strategies that remain relevant despite the changing job landscape. This focus on enduring tactics sets Blake apart as a thought leader in the field.

- **Research-Driven Insights**: A hallmark of Blake's work is the reliance on extensive research, ensuring that every piece of advice is grounded in data and real-world experience. This research-driven approach lends a level of credibility and depth to Blake's writings.

- **Commitment to Accessibility**: Recognizing the diversity of the workforce, Blake's writing is characterized by its accessibility, catering to individuals at various stages of their career, across industries and backgrounds.

Contributions to the Field

- **Publications and Articles**: Beyond "Evergreen Employment," Blake has authored numerous articles and papers, contributing valuable insights to leading journals and industry publications.

- **Speaking Engagements and Workshops**: A regular speaker at conferences and seminars, Blake shares expertise on career resilience, adaptability in job markets, and emerging employment trends.

- **Mentorship and Coaching**: Blake is passionate about mentorship, providing guidance to aspiring professionals and fellow career development experts. This mentorship extends beyond professional advice, encompassing holistic career and life planning.

Personal Philosophy and Interests

- **Lifelong Learning Advocate**: A firm believer in continuous personal and professional development, Blake embodies the principle of lifelong learning, constantly exploring new trends and expanding expertise.

- **Community Involvement**: Committed to giving back, Blake is actively involved in community initiatives focused on career education and skill development for underrepresented populations.

- **Avid Reader and Travel Enthusiast**: Outside of professional pursuits, Blake is an avid reader, finding inspiration in literature and philosophy. Travel is another passion, believing that exposure to different cultures and environments enriches one's perspective.

Conclusion

In "Evergreen Employment," Morgan E. Blake does not just offer a guide to navigating the job market; it presents a comprehensive approach to career development, underpinned by years of experience and a profound understanding of the employment landscape. Blake's anonymity allows the wisdom and guidance within the pages to resonate purely on their merit, making this book a valuable asset for anyone at any stage of their career journey.

Summary

www.ingramcontent.com/pod-product-compliance
Lightning Source LLC
Chambersburg PA
CBHW071055290526
45795CB00004B/1501